Copyright © 2025 by Alicia Davis

All rights reserved. This book or any portion thereof may not be reproduced or used in any manner whatsoever without the express written permission of the publisher except for the use of brief quotations in a book review.

Printed in the United States of America

First Edition, 2025

HARDBACK ISBN 979-8-3485-1701-4
PAPERBACK ISBN 979-8-3485-1699-4
EBOOK ISBN 979-8-3485-1700-7

Red Pen Edits and Consulting, LLC
www.redpeneditsllc.com

Welcome to Fearless & Focused: Affirmations to Build Strength, Confidence, and Courage!

This book is here to help you grow into the strong, brave, and confident person you're meant to be.

At Kadyn's Kandies, we believe that you have the power to do amazing things. This book is filled with positive affirmations, short, powerful reminders to keep you focused and fearless, no matter what challenges come your way. Whether you're trying something new, working hard on a goal, or need more confidence, these words will remind you of how strong you are.

Each affirmation is designed to help you stay strong when things get tough, keep your focus when things try to get in the way, and build the courage to go after your dreams. Remember, you can do anything you set your mind to, and these affirmations are here to help you feel ready for whatever comes next!

Read these words every day and get ready to take on the world with confidence, strength, and a fearless attitude.

You've got everything it takes to reach your goals!

I am proud of who I am and where I come from.

I am proud of my roots, my culture, and my heritage. My ancestors have paved the way for me, and I honor their strength by being the best version of myself.

I am strong, inside and out.

I know that true strength comes from within. My mind, body, and heart are all strong, and I use that strength to face challenges and keep moving forward with courage.

I am confident in who I am becoming.

I am always growing, learning, and becoming a better version of myself. Each day is a chance to improve, and I am excited about the man I am becoming.

I am capable of achieving my dreams.

There is no dream too big for me. I believe in my abilities, and I know that with hard work and determination, I can make my dreams come true.

I have the power to create change.

I am a force for good in this world. My actions, words, and ideas have the power to make a positive difference in my community and beyond.

I am confident in who I am becoming.

I am always growing, learning, and becoming a better version of myself. Each day is a chance to improve, and I am excited about the man I am becoming.

I believe in my abilities and my potential.
I know that I have endless potential. I believe in my talents and my skills, and I trust that I can accomplish anything I set my mind to.

I am worthy of respect and kindness.
I expect respect because I know my worth. I treat others with kindness and expect to be treated with the same respect I give.

I am smart, and my ideas matter.
My brain is powerful. I am intelligent, and my ideas are valuable. I am not afraid to speak up, because my voice matters.

I will never give up, no matter the challenge.
Even when things get tough, I remember that I am strong enough to keep going. Challenges are just opportunities for me to grow stronger.

I am deserving of all the good things life has to offer.
I deserve success, happiness, and love. I know that I am worthy of the best that life has to offer, and I am open to receiving all the good things that come my way.

I am a leader in my community and in my school.
I was born to lead. Whether it's in school, on the court, or in my community, I lead by example with respect, integrity, and kindness.

I respect myself and expect others to do the same.

Self-respect is the foundation of everything. I stand tall, proud of who I am, and expect others to treat me with the same respect I give to them.

I choose positivity over negativity.

I decide how I feel, and I choose to stay positive. I let go of negativity and focus on the good things in my life. My attitude shapes my future.

I am brave, and I take risks.

I am not afraid to try new things. I know that being brave means stepping out of my comfort zone and taking risks that will help me grow.

I am a problem-solver and a thinker.

When challenges arise, I know I can figure them out. I am a thinker and a problem-solver, and I will always find a way to succeed.

I will not let fear stop me from succeeding.
Fear is just a feeling, and I don't let it control me. I use my courage to push past fear and keep moving toward my goals.

I am a king in the making.
I am destined for greatness. Every decision I make, every step I take, brings me closer to becoming the man I am meant to be.

I am proud of my culture and my identity.

My culture is rich with history, pride, and strength. I carry it with me wherever I go, and I honor it by being the best version of myself.

I will never stop learning and growing.

I know that knowledge is power, and I am committed to learning every day. Whether in school, through books, or life experiences, I am always growing.

I was created on purpose and with purpose.

God made me for a special reason. I have unique gifts, talents, and abilities that are part of God's plan for me. Every day, I am part of something bigger, and I am important just the way I am.

I am kind, and I spread kindness to everyone I meet.

Kindness is a superpower, and I use it every day. I treat everyone with respect, regardless of who they are, because I know kindness always makes the world better.

I believe in myself and my dreams, even when others don't.
I trust my vision and believe in my dreams, even if others doubt me. My dreams are mine to chase, and I will follow them no matter what.

I am determined to overcome any obstacle in my way.
No matter what obstacles I face, I am determined to rise above them. I know that nothing is too hard for me to handle, and I will keep moving forward.

I am grateful for the opportunities in my life.
I am thankful for all the opportunities I have to grow, learn, and succeed. I don't take anything for granted and make the most of every chance I get.

I am a positive influence on the people around me.
My actions inspire others. I know that I have the power to uplift my friends, family, and community, and I choose to lead with positivity and strength.

I am proud of every step I take, no matter how small.
Each step I take toward my goals is an achievement. I am proud of my progress, whether it's a small victory or a big one, because every step counts.

I honor my past and create my own future.
I carry the strength and wisdom of my ancestors with me, but I am also the creator of my own future. I will make my story one of success, greatness, and impact.

I take responsibility for my actions and my future.
I am responsible for the choices I make, and I know that the decisions I make today shape my tomorrow. I take ownership of my actions and their consequences.

I am capable of great things, and I will never stop striving for my best.
I know that I am capable of achieving greatness. I will always strive for the best version of myself and work hard to reach my fullest potential.

I will never settle for less than my best.

I expect greatness from myself. I will not settle for mediocrity because I know I have the ability to do amazing things when I give my best effort.

I am a king, and my crown is already waiting for me.

I was born with greatness inside me. My journey is one of power, strength, and wisdom, and I know that I am destined to wear my crown proudly.

Congratulations!

You've made it through Fearless & Focused!

You are now filled with powerful words that will help you grow stronger, more confident, and braver every day.

Remember, the positive thoughts you've read are more than just words. They are reminders of the amazing strength and courage that already live inside you. Whenever you face a challenge, need more courage, or just want to remind yourself how awesome you are, you can always come back to
read these affirmations.

Keep using the words within this book to stay focused on your goals, be brave in everything you do, and never stop believing in yourself.

The world needs your strength, your heart, and your unique skills, so keep shining bright and pushing forward!

You are fearless.

You are focused.

You are capable of achieving great things!

Fearless and Focused

Coloring Pages

About The Author
Kadyn Gillie

Kadyn Gillie, the daughter of Kim Gillie and Alicia Davis, is a native of Barnwell, SC, and the CEO and founder of Kadyn's Kandies LLC, a thriving business she launched at the age of 6. What began as a candy company has since blossomed into a brand that includes children's toys, accessories, Kadyn's Kandy Tees, and stylish items for moms and dads. Kadyn's mission is to spread beauty, boldness, and kindness, one treat at a time one child at a time. She is dedicated to inspiring children to believe in their potential while embracing confidence, kindness, and creativity.

As a young entrepreneur, Kadyn continues to shine as a role model in her community and beyond, growing her brand while staying true to her mission. Looking toward the future, Kadyn dreams of becoming an illustrator, combining her creativity with her entrepreneurial spirit. Whether through her business or her art, Kadyn is committed to uplifting others, fostering a sense of possibility, and creating a world filled with smiles and empowerment.

www.ingramcontent.com/pod-product-compliance
Lightning Source LLC
LaVergne TN
LVHW070434080526
838201LV00132B/271